BLOOD-FEEDING BUGS AND BEASTS

BY L. PATRICIA KITE

The Millbrook Press
Brookfield, Connecticut

This book is dedicated to the wonderful Jerry Raney.

Photographs courtesy of Peter Arnold, Inc.: cover (© Hans Pfletschinger), pp. 1 (© David Scharf), 28 (© Gunter Ziesler), 29 (© Gunter Ziesler), 36 (© David Scharf), 39 (bottom: © Hans Pfletschinger); © Edward Ross: pp. 8, 11, 13 (top), 16, 19, 20, 35; Science Photo Library/Photo Researchers: pp. 13 (bottom), 22 (Cath Wadforth); Bruce Coleman Inc., NY: p. 17 (© Frith); Photo Researchers: p. 21 (© Larry Mulvehill); © Ron West/Nature Photography: pp. 31, 32, 33, 39 (top left and right).

Library of Congress Cataloging-in-Publication Data
Kite, L. Patricia.
Blood-feeding bugs and beasts / by L. Patricia Kite.
    p.   cm.
Includes bibliographical references (p.   ) and index.
Summary: Presents information about such creatures as lice, fleas, ticks, flies, and vampire bats.
ISBN 1-56294-599-8 (lib. bdg.)
1. Bloodsucking animals—Juvenile literature. 2. Bloodsucking insects—Juvenile literature. [1. Bloodsucking insects. 2. Insects.] I. Title.
QL756.55.K57   1995
591.53—dc20   95-19736
                                                    CIP   AC

Published by The Millbrook Press, Inc.
2 Old New Milford Road, Brookfield, Connecticut 06804

CONTENTS

More than 97 percent of world insects are helpful to people. Less than 3 percent are a nuisance.

Scientists estimate there are one million insect species. More will probably be discovered. Maybe you, or someone you know, will discover a new insect.

Blood-Feeding Bugs and Beasts may just be the start of your insect studies. Or, you may decide to learn more about bats, leeches, or ticks. Words that may be new to you are *italicized*. Definitions of those words appear in the Glossary on page 44.

As you study animal science, you will see Latin or Greek names used. The chapter called Scientific Names on page 41 helps you to understand these scientific names for future use.

You may want to research other blood-feeding insects, or different

FOREWORD

types of insects. See the section called Further Reading on page 46, visit your local library, and talk to a science teacher. An adult can help you find the telephone number of your nearest County Agricultural Extension department, or university entomology department.

Researching interesting science is the way many *entomologists* began their career.

Have fun!
Pat Kite

BLOOD-FEEDING BUGS AND BEASTS

This particular conenose is called a "kissing bug" because it occasionally will bite around the mouth of a sleeping person.

Most assassin bugs are beneficial. They assassinate or kill pest insects. But a few close relations, such as the conenoses, are blood feeders. Some nicknames for conenoses are "Texas bed bugs," "Mexican bed bugs," "kissing bugs," "masked bed bug hunter," "the big bed bug hunter," and "the big bed bug."

Conenoses need blood meals in order to grow. They usually feed on small animals, such as wood rats. But sometimes they enter homes. During the day, conenose bugs hide in wall cracks or similar places.

ASSASSIN BUGS

Conenoses usually come out to feed at night. Depending on the type of conenose, a person may not feel the bite, or it may be quite painful.

In tropical areas, such as Central and South America, conenoses can carry the extremely tiny *protozoan* which causes Chagas's disease. They pick up this protozoan from feeding on infected animals. North American conenoses don't usually *transmit* human diseases.

9

The term "bed bug" is believed to come from the old English word "bogy" or "hobgoblin," meaning "a terror in the dark."

Native American Indians had no bed bugs. These bloodsucking insects arrived in the New World with European colonists in the cracks of their wooden sailing ships.

BED BUGS

In Germany, bed bugs were called *Wandlausen* or "wall lice." In Egypt, one word for bed bug was *akalan*, or "an itching." In France, the bed bug was called *la punaise*, usually translated as "stinker." In North America, bed bugs may have regional nicknames such as mahogany flats, chinch bugs, and redcoats.

Bed bugs live and multiply in wall cracks and similar places. Their bite causes intense itching. They have stink glands which give off an unpleasant sweet smell.

Bed bugs do not have wings. They travel from one place to another on used furniture, in suitcases, on laundry, and on anything else on which they can hitch a ride. Rich and poor get them. At one time in England there were "de-

Unfed, the bed bug is about ⅕ inch long (5 millimeters), brown, oval, and flat. When well-fed it is red, rounded, and long. People once thought fed and unfed bed bugs were two different insects.

stroyers of vermin" who worked for "upperclasses" only. Royalty were among their regular customers.

The bed bug has beaklike mouthparts. These include a blood-sucking tube. Bed bug saliva contains a substance that stops blood from clotting. The bite is painless. A bed bug feeds for 3 to 10 minutes if not disturbed. Bed bug bites do not cause disease.

Male and female bed bugs suck blood. Females can't lay eggs until they get a blood meal. Once fed, each female deposits about 200 eggs during her lifetime.

Bed bugs avoid light. They find food by its body warmth. A sleeping person in a dark room is an ideal meal.

Try to catch a flea. Bounce, off it goes. In one record-breaking leap, a tiny flea jumped to a height of 8 inches (20 centimeters) and a distance of 13 inches (33 centimeters). If a flea were as big as a school child, bouncing over a 30-story–high building would be easy.

Almost any warm-blooded animal can be home to a flea. Dogs, cats, pigeons, rats, bats, squirrels, and humans are among the dining tables for over 1,000 worldwide flea types.

Nor are fleas picky eaters. A cat flea will bite a dog. A rat flea will bite a squirrel. And almost any type of flea will bite a human being if its usual meal animal isn't around.

FLEAS

Each flea has three hollow, needlelike piercing-sucking mouthparts. With these, a flea makes a tiny hole in an animal's skin. The flea begins sucking up blood. Its saliva contains a substance that stops blood from clotting before the flea finishes its meal.

Some people are more sensitive to this *anticoagulant* than others. Allergic people get small, red, itchy spots from flea bites.

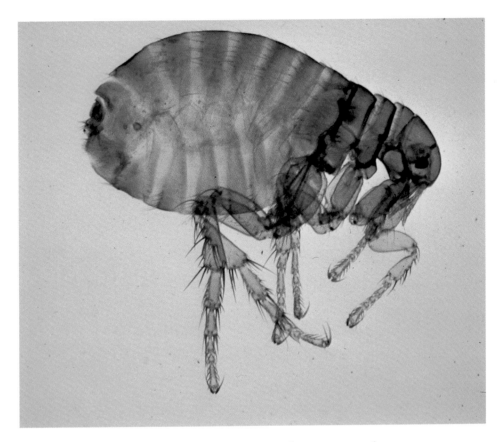

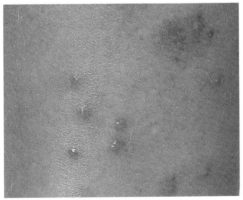

This picture of a common European or human flea has been magnified about 30 times its actual size. Such fleas are usually about 1/8 of an inch (3 millimeters) long and appear as little black specks to the human eye. A flea bite can cause red itchy spots on humans.

*F*orty million years ago, when a giant woolly mammoth stomped by, there were fleas waiting for it, too!

Flea bites can make people sick, although this doesn't happen too often anymore. But from the 14th to the 17th century, Europe was overrun with rats. Some rats carried a disease called bubonic plague. Bacteria-carrying hungry rat fleas moved from sick rats to humans. In 300 years, 25 million people died from what was called the "Black Death." Plague still occurs in many parts of the world today, although the United States has very few cases.

*T*he word "quarantine" comes from the Italian word *quaranta*, which means "forty." In the Middle Ages, to keep the plague from spreading, officials in many seaports ruled that passengers arriving on foreign ships had to wait 40 days before leaving the ship. They didn't know plague was carried by rat fleas, but *quaranta* still worked. In 40 days, anybody with plague aboard an *infested* ship would be dead. Burial was at sea.

There are at least 300 different *species* of leeches worldwide. Not all suck blood, but most do. Some leeches can bite through a hippopotamus hide. One species lives off the blood of young penguins, and another lives on the gums of the Nile crocodile.

Leeches live just about everywhere that gets damp. They can be found on high mountains, in polar seas, and in desert water holes.

People in the United States most often become a leech meal while swimming or playing in infested water. Leeches may sense the ripples and swim over.

LEECHES

Leeches range in size from ¼ inch (6 millimeters) to over 12 inches (30 centimeters) long. The giant Amazonia Leech can stretch to 18 inches (46 centimeters).

Some of the bloodsucking leeches have 80 sawlike teeth. The bite leaves a clear Y-shaped mark. Other leech types suck blood through a strawlike *proboscis*. A leech can suck up 10 times its weight in blood within half an hour. When the leech is full, it drops off.

*This closeup makes it easy to see that a
leech is a distant relative of the earthworm.
It is made up of ringlike sections, and the leech
moves by stretching and shortening its body.*

Hundreds of years ago, doctors believed using leeches to remove blood cured many medical problems. Some people actually made a living collecting leeches from ponds to sell to doctors.

About 1900, leech use in medicine just about stopped. But modern doctors have begun using leeches again. The saliva of some leeches contains a substance that prevents or dissolves blood clots that could interfere with human blood circulation. In the medicinal leech, this anticlotting substance is called hirudin.

Bloodsucking leeches are also being used in some microsurgery. Their feeding helps decrease blood-caused swelling in areas of poor circulation.

In 1984, a leech breeding center, Biopharm, was set up in Swansea, Wales. Medicinal leeches are raised in special tanks in dark, temperature-controlled rooms. Biopharm supplies many of the leeches used worldwide in hospitals and for biomedical research.

A leech looks very different when it is well fed. It takes on a mounded shape, engorged with the blood of its victim.

Many blood-feeding ticks cling to grasses and shrubs waiting to attach themselves to any passing meal.

Neither male nor female ticks can keep growing without blood meals, so both are eager hunters. Mouthparts are adapted for piercing, then tearing skin to find blood vessels. Dog ticks often feed in a dog's ears, between **TICKS** its toes, and on its back. On people, a favorite feeding site is at the back of the head. Hair tends to hide the tick.

Ticks fasten themselves to the host animal with their mouthparts. This attachment is reinforced with a cementlike *secretion*. Forcible attempts to detach a tick usually remove only its body. The mouthparts remain.

Ticks are very small, at least to start with. A brown dog tick is flat and just ⅛ inch (3 millimeters) long before feeding. It becomes a ½-inch- (12½-millimeter-) long roundish gray ball when filled with blood.

Although they look very different, the tick at the lower right was the same size as the others before it began its meal. A tick swells up to several times its former size when it becomes engorged with the blood of its victim.

Depending on type, a tick may feed over a few hours or over several days. After a full blood meal, the tick drops off its host to digest its food before feeding again.

After a full meal, an adult female tick begins egg laying. Each female may produce from 1,000 to 6,000 eggs at one

This female tick is only about half finished with her egg laying. The eggs will hatch into larvae. The larvae will attach themselves to passing animals to feed on blood and continue their development to adulthood.

time, depositing them on the ground or in debris. Tick larvae ("seed ticks") and nymphs also feed on blood.

Tick bites are not usually painful, so they may go unnoticed. Some tick bites leave a bright red spot. Sensitive people may feel some irritation.

Ticks run second to mosquitoes as *vectors* of human disease. Their salivary glands also secrete *toxins* or *venoms* or both. Depending on tick type, diseases and infections transmitted include: Colorado tick fever, tick paralysis, Rocky Mountain spotted fever, Q fever, St. Louis encephalitis, tularemia, relapsing fever, and Lyme disease.

Early spring to late summer is prime tick time. To avoid tick bites when in tick territory:

- Use wide paths so you stay away from shrubbery.
- Wear long pants and long-sleeved shirts. Tuck in shirt tails and tuck pant legs into your socks.
- Talk to your doctor about tick repellent.
- After being outdoors, check your body for ticks. Wash clothing.
- Learn safe methods of tick removal.

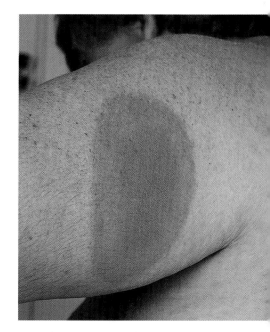

Early treatment can easily cure Lyme disease, so it is important to recognize the characteristic bull's eye rash that occurs after a tick bite.

Ticks are not insects but cousins to spiders and scorpions. Although a young tick has six legs, the adult tick has eight legs. All insects have six legs.

A color enhanced micro-graph, magnified 30 times, of a human head louse crawling over human hair.

At any time, 6 to 12 million Americans may have head lice, with most cases in children ages 1 to 12. Head scratching is the first symptom. Then you see louse eggs, or nits. Nits are grayish-white dots on hair, like sprinkled salt. Sometimes they look like dandruff. But dandruff brushes off easily. Nits don't.

Adult lice hide in hair. Lice have mouthparts for piercing skin and sucking up blood. The bite results in itching. While on a head, each sesame-seed-size female louse puts out about 100 to 350 eggs in her lifetime. She also produces a gluelike substance, so eggs stick firmly to hair.

HEAD LICE

The young lice hatch in about a week. Within three weeks they are creating more lice. In two months, a scientist calculated that a single female and her daughters can account for 112,778 new lice. The young feed on blood almost immediately after hatching. If they don't, they die.

Lice don't have wings. They don't hop, either. But they do crawl quickly. The grayish- to

*H*undreds of years ago, just about everybody had head lice. Gentlemen shaved their heads and wore wigs so they could get rid of lousiness by taking the wigs off.

reddish-brown louse usually gets about by head-to-head contact. It is also transferred by hairbrushes, clothing, seat covers, stuffed animals, and stereo headphones. Its clawlike grip allows it to hang on despite ordinary hair washing or brushing.

Long ago, lice were hard to get rid of. Today, a parent can ask a doctor, the school nurse, or a pharmacist about medicated shampoos. People also still use special fine-tooth combs, called nit combs, to get nits off the hair. Today's combs are plastic or sometimes metal. Nit combs made of boxwood, ivory, and bone have been found in burial sites from 9,000 years ago.

You may have heard someone called a "nit picker." It means someone who looks for tiny mistakes.

*T*here are several thousand lice species. Of these, there are about 560 bloodsucking species that live only on animals. Each type usually sticks to a specific animal. Humans have three types of lice. They are head lice, body lice (sometimes called "cooties"), and pubic lice, also called "crabs."

In 1968, a Swiss entomologist discovered a bloodsucking moth. It lives in Malaysia, India, and Sri Lanka.

Most moths feed on flower *nectar*. These moths have a long, soft proboscis, or feeding tube. It is kept curled during flight. When the moth lands on a flower, the proboscis unrolls. It enters the flower center to suck up nectar.

In some areas of the world, nectar isn't available at all times. To survive, moth types living in those areas have adapted over many generations.

VAMPIRE MOTHS

For example, a few moth species have developed proboscis strong enough to pierce the peel of soft, decaying fruit. This lets the moth feed on fruit juices. The proboscis of one fruit-feeding moth is even stiff enough to puncture the peel of a fresh orange.

But the vampire moth has developed the strongest proboscis of all. Not only can it pierce fresh fruit, it can puncture the skin of local animals, including cattle, water buffalo, and deer.

After making the puncture, the moth very rapidly moves its head from side to side. Its proboscis has barbs. The rapid head vibration enables it to drill into the blood stream. Blood is then sucked up through the proboscis. The vampire moth may feast on the animal for up to an hour.

Forty-two species of bats have been sighted in North America, and not one feeds on blood. Most bats eat an enormous number of insects, sometimes more than 100 per night per bat. Other food includes fruit, fish, and plant nectar.

There are only three kinds of vampire bats. They all live in tropical Central and South America. Of these, one prefers bird blood, another feeds on birds and animals, and one just on animals. That one is the "common vampire bat." It lives in caves.

VAMPIRE BATS

The reddish-brown body of the vampire bat is about the size of a sparrow. Its tiny triangular front teeth are razor sharp.

Vampire bat bites are usually painless. The bat feeds at night when animals sleep. With a silent, swift movement, the bat's sharp teeth scoop out tiny pieces of skin. An anticoagulant in bat saliva keeps blood flowing.

Many people think that bats suck blood out of their victims, but they don't. The lower lip curls to make a funnel. Then the bat quickly

Despite its fierce look and threatening reputation, the vampire bat is surprisingly small. An adult is typically about 3 inches (8 centimeters) long and weighs about an ounce (28 grams).

laps up blood with its long tongue. A bat can lap up about one tablespoon (15 milliliters) of blood per night.

The victim is not hurt by the bite itself, which soon heals. Nor does the small blood loss cause harm. The problem is with the bat's saliva. Bats, whether vampire or not, if infected, can transmit rabies. It is best to admire wild bats, but not handle them.

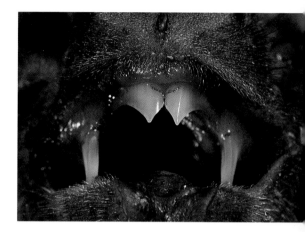

The teeth of a vampire bat are made for piercing, not chewing. The bat's esophagus is short and narrow and will only allow the animal to swallow fluids.

Are you interested in learning more about bats? Write Bat Conservation International, 500 North Capital of Texas Highway, Austin, Texas 78746, or the National Bat Center (NBC) at 5721 Randolph Road, Rockville, Maryland 20804. NBC, a non-profit organization, says new bat information groups are forming all the time, and there may be one near you. Send a self-addressed stamped envelope for a prompt reply.

Some people think bats are lucky. The Chinese symbol for *fu* (bat) is the same as the symbol for happiness. In the Chinese tradition, seeing a bat foretells good luck and long life.

Although the common house fly neither bites or stings, there are many types of bloodsucking flies.

Biting Stable Fly. There's a story that biting stable flies helped speed up the signing of America's Declaration of Independence. Back in 1776, Independence Hall in Philadelphia wasn't too far **FLIES** from where cattle grazed. On days when it looks like rain, stable flies often seek shelter in people buildings.

Inside Independence Hall, the signers of the Declaration kept arguing about the document's exact wording. But once stable flies entered the room, and started biting these famous men right through their silk stockings, the squabbling ceased. "Let's get on with it," said one, "and get out of here." So they did.

Stable flies are found every place in the world where there are garbage dumps, barnyards, pastures, and coastlines. Both male and female feed on flower nectar as well as animal blood.

Stable flies look like house flies, but their mouthparts aren't soft and spongy. Stable fly mouthparts are hard and stick out in front like a bayonet. The stable fly stabs its victim, often on the legs. The stab is quite painful, but feeding does not transmit diseases among people.

A look-alike of the common house fly, the biting stable fly has the same single pair of wings and 3-part body made up of the head, the thorax, and the abdomen. The difference lies in the sharp parts hidden in the mouth of the biting fly.

Deer Fly. Deer flies like open woodland and wooded pastures near streams.

Only female deer flies bite. In addition to animals, they tend to bite people around the forehead, eyebrows, and back of neck. On occasion, they can transmit bacteria that cause tularemia in people.

The deer fly has been known to transmit tularemia, an infectious disease characterized by high fever. Mosquito repellents appear to be effective in fending off deer flies as well.

Only the female horse fly sucks blood. We can tell that this fly is a female because the eyes of the male are even larger and appear to be connected at the top of the head.

American Horse Fly. American horse flies are large. Some types get up to 1 $\frac{1}{8}$ inches (almost 3 centimeters) long. The largest horse flies can move as fast as 30 miles (48 kilometers) an hour.

O f the ten plagues of Egypt mentioned in the Old Testament, at least two of the plagues, and maybe even four, were caused by fly-transmitted diseases.

Males feed on flower nectar and pollen. Females feed on blood. Head, neck, back, or shoulders are favorite feeding sites. Horse flies don't stick to horses, cattle, or hogs. In many parts of the world, lizards, turtles, elephants, and hippopotamuses—and people—are among their victims.

Black Fly. Tiny black flies or "Buffalo Gnats," appear by the thousands in late spring around shaded flowing waters. Only the female bites. This bite is not painful right away. But within an hour, there's a lot of pain, swelling, and itching.

Black flies do not transmit disease in North America. But in tropical countries, they carry a nematode that causes a form of blindness. Black flies bite in the daylight only. They prefer to crawl into sleeves, under neck bands, and just beneath hat rims.

Tsetse Fly. Tsetse flies exist only in tropical Africa. One species transmits the dreaded African sleeping sickness to people and cattle. After sucking blood from an infected animal or person, the fly carries parasites causing sleeping sickness to its next victims. Affected persons feel very ill and extremely sleepy. They eventually die.

The tsetse flies that spread sleeping sickness live mostly around river banks and lake shores. People and animals often cannot live in infested areas.

Both male and female tsetse flies suck blood. Their mouthparts are long and piercing enough to bite through heavy clothing.

Tsetse flies look different from other flies: They fold their wings over their backs.

Unlike most other fly species, the female tsetse fly produces only one egg at a time. The larva hatches within the female's body where it remains until fully grown. Then the female deposits it on the ground. It immediately turns into a pupa. A winged adult emerges about a month later.

"T se" is an African word for fly. Saying "Tsetse" emphasizes the nastiness of these particular flies. If you want to say "tsetse fly" correctly, just say "tsetse."

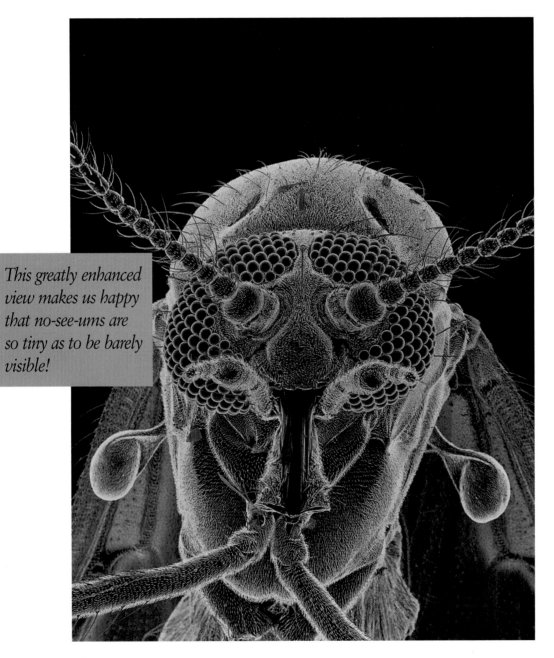

This greatly enhanced view makes us happy that no-see-ums are so tiny as to be barely visible!

The Marines at one naval base called biting midges "flying teeth." Other regional nicknames include "no-see-ums," "punkies," "sand flies," "sand fleas," "black gnats," and "moose flies."

Biting midges are very small or "midget" flies. They feed on all types of animals. Some suck blood from dragonflies, caterpillars, mosquitoes, and even earthworms.

Females tend to be vicious biters. Each female may need up to four blood meals before she can lay eggs. She won't go away until she has gotten a meal.

NO-SEE-UMS

Tiny midges, about .06 inch (less than 3 millimeters) long, feed in groups of thousands, usually in the daylight. Midge mouthparts are piercing. Each bite stings. A small red mark at each bite site later swells and itches. A small clear blister may form.

After feeding, females place eggs in damp places. The newly hatched wormlike larvae eat the larvae of other insects.

Scientists have recently found a biting midge preserved in *amber.* It was 125 million years old.

More people are bitten by mosquitoes than by any other bloodsucking insect. Only the female mosquito bites. And it isn't really a bite. The female punctures skin with four needlelike barbed mouthparts.

A tubelike stylet sucks up blood. Within three minutes, a female mosquito has withdrawn her fill, as much as twice her weight.

Itchy red marks appear at the bite site. They are caused by an allergic reaction to the mosquito's saliva. Because this saliva contains an *anesthetic*, the victim does not feel the bite right away and smash the mosquito in the middle of its meal.

MOSQUITOES

There are 2,960 different species of mosquitoes. Not all are blood suckers. Some feed on flower nectar. A few feed on other mosquitoes. But most female mosquitoes have a need for blood meals. Among other victims, mosquitoes feed on deer, snakes, birds, and frogs. There is even a mosquito that feeds on a fish, the mud skipper.

If a female blood-feeding mosquito can't find an animal meal site, she'll feed on flower

A female mosquito can lay up to 300 eggs at one time (upper left). An egg develops into a wormlike larva (at left in upper right) and then, in a week or slightly longer, into a pupa (at right in upper right). Two to four days later, an adult mosquito emerges. At right is a mosquito engaged in feeding. Note that it is quite literally filled with blood—a mosquito is capable of sipping as much as twice her own weight at a single feeding.

The mosquito is a fly. Its name comes from the Spanish word for fly, *mosca*, or "little fly." One type of mosquito was around during the age of the dinosaurs.

nectar and plant juices. That's what the male mosquito eats. But without the protein in a blood meal, the female can't lay eggs.

Female mosquitoes deposit eggs in many places, including cold Arctic lakes, salt water marshes, and steaming deep tropical pools. Eggs are also placed in water-filled tires, tin cans, flowerpots, birdbaths, hollow tree stumps, and puddles.

Mosquito *larvae*, or young, are called "wigglers" because of their wiggly swimming pattern. Next they become *pupae*, more commonly called "tumblers" because they roll around and bounce up and down in water. Look for wigglers and tumblers in the next puddle you notice. During warm weather, a very small puddle can hold more than a thousand upcoming mosquitoes.

In some areas of the world, certain types of mosquitoes carry disease organisms in their saliva. Among the many mosquito-carried diseases are malaria, yellow fever, dengue, and encephalitis. In North America there are many public programs to eliminate mosquito breeding places. In other countries, this is more difficult to accomplish.

It is the carbon dioxide in exhaled breath that makes a mosquito visit a person. In pitch darkness, a mosquito can sense an animal 40 yards (36 meters) away.

Bats and leeches are usually easy to look up in reference books if you want more information about them. However if you want to learn more about insects, you may not always find them indexed under any of their common American names.

Instead, you may find members of CLASS Insecta indexed under a Greek or Latin scientific name or grouping.

The biggest grouping is the OR-DER. There are about 30 different orders. Every insect in a particular order has many characteristics, or features, that are the same.

For example: all FLEAS are in the order Siphonaptera. Fleas do not have wings. They are very small. They have hard dark bodies which are flat from side to side.

Another example: all sucking LICE are in the order Anoplura. Lice are tiny. Their abdomen is usually rounded.

A third example: all true FLIES are in the order Diptera. All true FLIES have one pair of wings, short antennae, and a soft body.

Because each ORDER contains so many Insects, scientists have divided each ORDER into many FAMILIES. The members of an insect family usually look and act somewhat alike. So, while each fly is in the order Diptera, the mosquito would be in a different family from the horse fly, no-see-um, or biting stable fly.

Mosquitoes are in the order Diptera and the family Culicidae.

Horse flies are in the order Diptera and the family Tabanidae.

No-see-ums are in the order Diptera and the family Ceratopogonidea.

Biting stable flies are in the order Diptera and the family Muscidae.

Tsetse flies are in the order Diptera and are usually placed in the family Glossinidae.

From here, scientists divide each insect FAMILY into GENERA (singular GENUS). Within each genus are many different insect SPECIES or types.

For example, there are about 85,000 different species of flies. Each species has a name. The first part of the name is the GENUS or general name, and the second part is the specific name. You see them both together.

Horse fly = order Diptera, family Tabanidae, genus Tabanus. There are many species of horse flies, including *Tabanus punctifer*, *Tabanus americanus*, *Tabanus trimaculatus*.

To make research easier for you, here are some other family or species names under which insects and animals featured in this book are commonly found in books for further reading:

Vampire moth = *Calpe eustrigata*
Bed bug = *Cimex lectularis*
Assassin Bug = *Reduviidae*
Ticks = *Argasidae* and/or *Ixodidae*
Deer Fly = *Tabanidae*

It takes a very long time, and lots of study, to understand all the order, family, genus, and species names for insects and other animals. Sometimes the name of an insect's or animal's discoverer is included too. But that's another adventure in learning.

Amber. A fossil resin, or thick liquid, secreted by pine trees, in which insects were often trapped.

Anesthetic. A substance that takes away body feeling or sensation.

Anticoagulant. A substance that stops or slows blood clotting.

Entomologist. A person who specializes in the study of insects.

Infested. Said of a location in which insects are present in great numbers, usually creating a problem.

Larva (plural *larvae*). Young emerging from insect eggs in grub, wormlike, or caterpillar form.

Nectar. A sweet fluid, made by flowers, which attracts insects.

Parasite. An animal or plant that feeds and lives on or in another animal or plant.

Proboscis. A tubelike insect mouthpart used for sucking or piercing.

Protozoan. A microscopic organism composed of one cell.

GLOSSARY

Pupa (plural *pupae*). A stage of insect growth between larva and adult.

Secretion. A specialized material formed by the body.

Species. Animals or plants with specific characteristics that distinguish them from others that may appear similar.

Toxin. A poison formed by a living organism.

Transmit. To carry from one place to another.

Vector. A carrier of a disease-producing organism.

Venom. A poisonous fluid formed by certain animals.

FURTHER READING

Barker, Will. *Familiar Insects of America*. New York: Harper and Brothers, 1960.

Burton, Maurice and Burton, Richard. *International Wildlife Encyclopedia*, Volume 6. New York: Marshall Cavendish, 1969.

Clausen, Lucy W. *Insect Fact and Folklore*. London: Macmillan, 1969.

Hanson, Jeanne K. *Of Kinkajous, Capybars, Horned Beetles, Seladangs*. New York: HarperCollins, 1991.

Klots, Alexander and Elsie Klots. *1001 Questions Answered About Insects*. New York: Dover Publications, 1977.

Milne, Lorus and Margery Milne. *Audubon Society Field Guide to North American Insects and Spiders*. New York: Knopf, 1986.

Scheffel, Richard L., ed. *ABC's of Nature*. Pleasantville, NY: Reader's Digest Association, 1984.

Watson, Allan, et al. *The Dictionary of Butterflys and Moths*. New York: McGraw-Hill, 1975.

Wood, Gerald L. *Animal Facts and Feats*. New York: Sterling, 1977.

World Book Encyclopedia. Chicago: Childcraft International, 1978, 1994.

Zim, Herbert S. and Cottam, Clarence. *Insects*. New York: Golden Press, 1956.

Page numbers in *italics* refer
to illustrations.

INDEX